How to *Sell MORE* in *LESS Time*

Tim Connor, CSP

How to *Sell MORE in LESS Time*

Copyright: 2000 Tim Connor, CSP

Library of Congress Catalogue No: In Publication.

All rights reserved under International and Pan American Copyright Conventions including reproductions in whole or in part in any form.

ISBN: 1-930376-18-9

Published by: Connor Resource Group

Cover Design: Melissa Lingle

Editor: Kristen Boykin

Manufactured in: The United States of America

First Printing: November 2000

For information on Tim's services as a meeting or convention speaker please call: 704-895-1230 • 704-895-1231 (fax) • ***800-222-9070*** 800-222-9071 (fax) E Mail: speaker@bellsouth.net. • Website: www.timconnor.com

"No one can manage time. Time passes. You can't store it up, use it again, slow it down or speed it up. All you can do is enjoy one precious moment at a time as the clock of life ticks relentlessly on."

Tim Connor, CSP

How to Sell More in Less Time

"It is not enough to get things done. They must be done right."
Arthur Hadley

Tim Connor, CSP

"*Time is the most valuable thing a man can spend.*
Diogenes

How to Sell More in Less Time

Books by Tim Connor...

Soft Sell

Win - Win Selling

The Voyage

Sales Mastery

The Trade - Off

The Ancient Scrolls

Daily Success Journal

The Road to Happiness

The Road to Happiness Fun-Book

Crossroads – A Love Story

Assignment Workbooks:

- *-Sales*
- *-Relationships*
- *-Success*
- *-Customer Service*
- *-Management*

Let's Get Back to Basics:

- *- Success*
- *- Sales*
- *- Relationships*
- *- Management*
- *- Motivation*
- *- Happiness*

Tim Connor, CSP

Contents...

Chapter One: 15
Personal values, beliefs and attitudes as they impact your time management

Chapter Summary: 65

Chapter Two: 67
Personal organization and your time and territory management

Chapter Summary: 106

Chapter Three: 108
Goals as they relate to your time and territory management

Chapter Summary: 134

Chapter Four: 136
Planning and time and territory management

Chapter Summary: 146

Chapter Five: 147
Common time and territory time wasters and stretchers

Chapter Summary: 157

Chapter Six: 158
Technology and time and territory management

Conclusion: 163
Your personal action plan

Recommended Reading: 167

How to Sell More in Less Time

> "The future is purchased by the present."
>
> **Samual Johnson**

Tim Connor, CSP

Introduction...

What is your time worth? Divide the number of hours you work by your income and you have it. What you are being paid for each hour of your day. Want to increase the number? Work longer hours or get better results from the hours you work. Simple enough? Yes and no. This book will give you the principles, tools, attitudes and techniques to increase your hourly value – thus your income.

The truth about time. For over 25 years I have been surveying audiences and clients the numbers have been consistent for all of that time. <u>*The question*</u>: How much of your total work time are you spending actually selling – on the phone or in person? This does not include:

-writing letters to prospects
-solving after sales problems
-travel time
-paperwork
-meetings
-proposals

Your answer:_____

My personal research over the years shows the typical salesperson spends 10-20 percent of their time selling and 70-80 percent doing everything else. Isn't it amazing that you can earn an income in sales spending less than 30 percent of your time selling? Imagine what you could do to your results and income if you could increase that number only 10 percent? How about 20% or even more?

How to Sell More in Less Time

Territory management and effective time use is a function of many skill and attitude; prejudices, attitudes, habits and personal philosophies. No one can manage time. If a person has a "time management" issue or problem it is most likely due to a weakness or lack of ability in some other area of their life i.e. managing - resources, people, decisions, problems, emotions, failure, activities, success etc.

In order to improve ultimate time effectiveness you must identify these tendencies, attitudes or weaknesses and then develop skills and attitudes to address and overcome them. You can't improve time use, it is a nebulous concept. I challenge anyone to manage the next minute or hour. Can't be done.

The only purpose of this book is to help you identify the attitudes, strengths, weaknesses, prejudices you have about time and management of your territory and give you the ideas and tools to improve or change. It will also help you:

-learn to get better use from the time you have at your disposal within the framework of your personal values, needs, responsibilities and roles.

-master new skills that will permit the better management of time and related challenges.

Effective time use can not be learned only in a seminar. The ideas, concepts, approaches and attitudes that impact a person's use of time will only change when you – self-discover the need for necessary changes – and then integrate these new skills and attitudes into your regular roles, responsibilities and philosophy.

Tim Connor, CSP

I also urge you to purchase a three ring binder to record your answers to the many questions and the insights you have as you move through the various topics.

Time Tip

Invest in an inexpensive stop-watch and keep track of your time use in the various areas of your life for two weeks.

Tim Connor, CSP

Territory Management:

Territory management, like time management, is a function of many attitudes, habits, values, skills and beliefs. It is also a function of:

-the geographic size of the territory

-the number of clients/prospects in the territory

-the method of travel through the territory i.e. air, car etc.

-the non-sales responsibilities within the territory.

-the degree of administrative sales support

In order to effectively manage a sales territory it is critical that a salesperson have a "prospecting strategy' – a rational for how much time, energy and resources to give to each type of prospects/customers. Many salespeople travel hundreds of unnecessary miles each week or month and still do not effectively 'cover' his/her territory. Without this prospecting strategy it is impossible to get better use of one's time and have effective territory coverage.

-My objectives are simple, to:

-give you the understanding of the importance of the relationship between attitude issues and time and territory management.

-give you the necessary awareness for time/territory changes in

How to Sell More in Less Time

areas where you feel adjustments will be beneficial.

-help you identify destructive personal and/or career time/territory attitudes/philosophies/patterns/habits and attitudes.

-give you new tools to improve in all areas where you need modification in time usage.

-reinforce time use/territory management skills and attitudes that are currently effective for you.

-share a variety of time/activity/territory management ideas you can use, given the constraints of your position, roles responsibilities and available support staff.

-help you recognize where your time use/territory management is out of control due to other people or outside influences.

Tim Connor, CSP

Chapter 1...

Personal values, beliefs, attitudes and philosophy as they relate to your time and territory management.

Overview:

-Time and Territory management defined

The keys to improving time use and territory management – are to:

-know yourself

-know your tendencies

-know your strengths

-know your weaknesses

-know your goals

-identify your common time wasters

-have a prospecting strategy

-establish regular planning times

-be ruthless with your self-discipline

How to Sell More in Less Time

Territory management is the ability to maximize your results, reach your goals and effectively build your business in your territory while satisfying the demands and expectations of your management team and current customers.

Life and time is a perceptual experience.

No one looks at life; its events, conditions or circumstances the same. We see life not as it is, but as we are. Each of us has a mental filter through which we interpret other people's behavior, events and circumstances. Ten people can look at the same piece of art, auto accident, movie or sunset and see it differently. This gives life is diversity and its uniqueness. Time also is a perceptual issue. When you are doing what you like time seems to fly. When you are doing something you dislike it seems to crawl.

Our perceptions are also a major issue when it comes to motivating ourselves on a consistent basis to use time wisely. If we fail to perceive life and its events and people clearly we will tend to fall into a number of de-motivating traps such as; guilt, blame, resentment, anger and any number of other negative emotions or feelings, and these all take mental time and focus which tends to take your eye of the critical tasks at hand. These negative responses will color your use of your talent, and how you treat others on a regular basis as well as how you use your time and manage your territory.

Where are your perceptions about life, people, events, circumstances, your past, present, time or future clouded? Where do you need a clearer vision and more accurate perceptual integrity?

Tim Connor, CSP

-The issue of procrastination

Procrastination is the number one cause of poor time use. It is best defined as the fear of the unknown. It is putting things off, like - decisions, actions, problem solving, until a more perceived favorable time in the future. Until you master procrastination you will never effectively be able to manage your time and territory effectively and/or successfully. Here are a few questions concerning procrastination:

1. Do you consider yourself a procrastinator?

2. Do you work best under pressure?

3. In what areas of your life or career do you typically procrastinate?

4. Why?

5. Do you tend to avoid difficult people or decisions?

6. Why?

7. Do you often postpone actions that will require a lot of: time, energy, creativity, effort or patience?

8. How do you feel about other people who tend to procrastinate?

9. Are your goals clearly established?

10. Do you have time-frames for them?

Tim Connor, CSP

Start a procrastination log. Record everything you put off: Decisions, actions, difficult tasks, important phone calls, customer problems etc.

How to Sell More in Less Time

-Personal values and T/T management

Who you are will define your time/territory management more than any other factor. Your opinions, expectations, values, prejudices, conditioned beliefs as well as your attitudes about your past, present and future. Answer the following questions honestly.

1. Are you typically late with projects, assignments, or for appointments?

2. How do you feel about people who are late?

3. Do you find yourself often rushing?

4. Are you a workaholic?

5. Do you look forward to Friday's or Monday's?

6. Are you an early or late riser?

7. Are you a morning or evening person?

8. Do you consider your life balanced and in harmony or out of balance?

9. Where are you out of balance and why?

-Developing a working philosophy of time/territory management

What exactly is a philosophy of time and territory management?

Your philosophy about time will ultimately determine whether you use your time wisely and effectively manage your territory. A person's philosophies contribute to his or hers beliefs, values, expectations and outcomes. For example, one philosophy of time is that there is never enough. Another is an over optimistic realization of what you can accomplish in any given time segment. How would you describe or define your philosophy of time?

-Know your prime time

What is prime time? It is that time of the day, week or month when you are at your best. Are you a morning person? Late night person?

Other? Does your energy fade during a certain time of the day or week?

How about your Prime Time PLUS- This is that combination of time when you are at your best and your customers/prospects can see you. For example if you are a morning person and a client/prospect wants a conference call in the morning- this is your Prime Time Plus. However if you are an afternoon person (your energy, creativity, imagination) peaks in the mid afternoon and you are not at your best in the early morning and a prospect wants a meeting in the morning this is not your Prime Time OR your Prime Time Plus. The key is to schedule critical sales activities during Prime Time Plus and non sales activities during you non Prime Time Plus.

What is your Prime Time?

What is your Prime Time Plus?

-Attitudes and time/territory management

What are some common time/territory management attitudes?

1. There is always tomorrow.

2. There is never enough time to do a good job.

3. I have too much on my plate.

4. There are too many demands made on my time.

5. There is too much paperwork.

6. I don't have enough time to waste time on good/bad prospects.

7. My geographic territory is too large.

8. I have too many prospects/customers.

9. I don't have anyone to delegate to.

10. I have to do it myself if it is going to be done right.

-Focus and concentration

The ability to concentrate is one of the critical traits of good time managers. Concentration is the ability to give 100 percent focus on an action, a project, assignment, decision or activity. This does not mean that other priorities are totally set aside. The ability to multi-task (chew gum and walk at the same time) is often necessary. However, when you try to write a letter while on hold with a prospect I guarantee that one or both will suffer.

Where or in what circumstances do you have difficulty concentrating?

Why?

How to Sell More in Less Time

Here are a few keys:

1. If you make lots of mistakes this could be sign you lack focus.

2. If you do not spend adequate time planning you may suffer in execution later.

3. We often pay the price of discipline or regret.

4. Periodically ask yourself: does this decision, project or activity have my full attention?

5. What is taking your eye off the ball on this activity?

6. If you are often late or unprepared this could be evidence of poor concentration.

7. Does your mind wander while in conversations with others?

8. Do you work in a cluttered environment?

9. Don't rush anything. Give it the time it deserves.

10. It often appears to be easier to do it again than to do it right the first time.

11. Do you often forget ideas or misplace where you put things frequently.

Tim Connor, CSP

-Expectations

Be careful what you focus on, you might just bring it into realty.

Many years ago there was a study done at a major university. The researchers wanted to determine if there was a relationship between expectations and outcomes. The result was called the Pygmalion Effect. In essence it found that: what you believe will come to pass (expectations as a result of your focus) will eventually become a reality.

<u>Let's use a practical business example to illustrate this phenomena. Take yourself back to 1988.</u>

-Housing starts were declining
-Interest rates were rising
-Lay-offs were beginning
-Unemployment was rising
-Businesses were cutting back
-The media focused on the negatives rather than the positives
-Negative word-of-mouth was increasing

BINGO......we have just talked ourselves into a full blown recession. Why? How? The Pygmalion Effect is in full swing.

Expecting negative outcomes changes your attitudes, actions and behavior. As a result your outcomes match your expectations because you tend to:

-focus on what's wrong
-concentrate on what you can't do rather than what you can
-talk about what's not working rather than what is

How to Sell More in Less Time

BINGO.......

-your business begins to decline
-people buy less
-inventories build
-sales decline

Can this all be avoided? Is there anything we can do to stop this downward spiral? The answer is YES. The economy has been ebbing and flowing (up and down) for over 100 years. In these down periods some people survive, some fail and some prosper. What is the difference in these outcomes? Everyone, regardless of their outcome are all operating in the same economic climate and they all have 24 hours a day at their disposal? The answer is – what are you focusing on, expecting, talking about and doing.

Regardless of what is going on out there – the economy/market place you and I can control what is going on in-here – our own mind.

Business may slow so you may have to:

-think differently

-act more creatively

-sell more aggressively

-work smarter

-think faster

-work harder

-get up earlier

-go to bed later

-react sooner

but in the end, because of these actions you will continue to get your share of whatever business is out there and beat the competition.

The opposite of this is a resignation that:

-there is nothing I can do
-it is out of my control
-the situation is inevitable
-you'll just have to wait it out hoping you make it through.

Refuse to turn your destiny over to:

-the economy
-government actions or decisions
-the weather
-or any other external circumstance or situation.

-Prioritizing

Establishing priorities is a difficult task for many people. They tend to give equal status to everything or they are unrealistic about their ability to get things done within a certain time-frame. Consider the following:

1. Do you always work from to-do lists?

How to Sell More in Less Time

2. Do you have a system of prioritizing prospects, customers, projects, tasks?

3. Do you tend to rate all of your tasks or "to-do's" equally important?

4. If you do prioritize, do you always complete the most important ones first or jump all around the list?

5. Do you tend to let outside influences determine your priorities?

6. Can you complete one task prior to starting another?

7. Are you realistic about your ability to complete a specific task in a specific time period?

8. Do you use your "down time" to catch up or do you fritter it away?

Tim Connor, CSP

Time Tip

Spend the next seven days keeping track of your routine activities and how much time they take i.e. reading the newspaper, lunch alone, travel, television, playing telephone tag etc.

How to Sell More in Less Time

Improve your AIM.

One of the critical elements for success in sales is to have the proper aim.

A - *Awareness* of what is, needs to change, or can be.

I - *Intent*. Having a clear focused intent to change, grow, develop or modify.

M - *Movement*. To have consistent movement or progress toward that is consistent with your intent.

As you reflect on your life as well as those who have crossed your path over the years, if you use the above word as a template: AIM, you will find that when you or most people have failed to hit the target it is because of one of these three causes:

A lack of awareness.
A lack of intent.
A Lack of positive consistent movement.

Here are 15 questions (5 for each item) to ask yourself to determine how you are doing in any or all areas of your life.

Awareness:

1. Do you know where you need improvement in any area of your life or are you in denial?

2. Have other's pointed out areas for improvement, but you have failed to accept their feedback?

3. Is there a nagging feeling in your gut that some area of your life could be better?

4. Do you pay attention to signals your body sends you on a regular basis?

5. Are you satisfied with your progress in all areas of your life?

Intent:

1. Do you give yourself or others excuses?

2. Do you let yourself of the hook when you fail to meet your goals?

3. Do you have an action plan or personal mission statement that guides you?

4. Have you 'settled for' in any area of your life?

5. Have you let others negatively impact your dreams and or desires?

Movement:

How to Sell More in Less Time

1. Do you track your progress regularly?

2. Do you reward your successes?

3. Do you break down you goals into smaller steps?

4. Do you make some progress every day?

5. Do you give up early or easily?

-Overcoming the fear of rejection

Why is the fear of rejection (an attitude) one of the critical time wasters in sales? Why do people let this fear negatively influence their behavior? Here are a few thoughts to consider.

1. Not everyone you try to sell to will want to buy from you.

2. Expecting everyone you meet to like or accept you is to live in fantasy-land.

3. If you don't ask for anything, something – it is unlikely you will ever get it.

4. The fear of rejection prevents you from asking probing questions, asking for an appointment, asking for the order.

5. The fear of rejection is one of the major causes of failure in all areas of life, not just sales.

6. The fear of rejection is an attitude issue and can only be overcome by strengthening other attitudes – such as confidence, self-belief, patience,
   trust, and your self-image.

7. The fear of rejection is not a skill issue and can't be overcome with the latest self-help technique or fad that force you to behave in ways that are not comfortable for you..

8. The fear of rejection is a symptom of a need for acceptance, approval or validation.

9. The fear of rejection sends a loud non-verbal message to the other person that you lack confidence or belief in; yourself, your product or service and/or your ability to help them or solve their problems.

Does the fear of rejection ever prevent you from:

1. Picking up the phone and making that next call?

2. Asking for the business?

3. Asking difficult probing questions?

4. Asking for referrals?

5. Asking for a bigger order?

6. Asking for a letter of testimony?

7. Asking for anything you want?

8. Asking for more responsibility in your position or a raise?

9. Following up on a customer who has had a problem?

10. Asking for an appointment with an important person?

11. Asking for a cash deposit?

12. Asking for a long-term contract?

13. Asking for_____ (you fill in the rest)

-Keep your focus in the present.

Each of us gets 86,400 moments a day, every day, every week until our last breath. Each of these moments is unique. From one second to the next we are not the same person. We learn something about ourselves or the world. We feel different emotions. We think different thoughts. We hear new sounds or we see new sights. Each moment, all 86,400 of them is precious. Because it is these moments one at a time that separate us from each other or bring us together, separate us from life or brings us closer to it. And separate us from life and death.

Tim Connor, CSP

So many salespeople spend much of these moments either in the past: Why didn't I? I wish I had. Why did I? Why didn't you or they? If only I......etc.etc.

Other's spend these moments in the future: Dreaming about what one day will be. What tomorrow will bring. What next week, year or someday will be about. Life is not lived in these past or future moments. You can't earn money tomorrow. You can't hug your child tomorrow. You can't tell your mother you love them tomorrow. And you can learn anything tomorrow. You do all of these things and millions more in the now moments one second at a time 86,400 times a day. They slip by at a rather quick pace. Life slips by before you know it. You are born...swish. You graduate from high school, swish. You marry, swish. You turn 50, swish. You retire, swish. You die. That's it in this life folks, the final swish. And the interesting thing is, the time between these swishes seems to fly by the older we get. One day you will realize that you have more life behind you than in front of you. Scary thought until you get used to it.

All it takes for many people to wake up to the gift of each now moment is the - death of a loved one, an illness that brings them close to the end, but spares them, or even a new gray hair or extra pound or two. The loss of a close friend. The loss of a dear relative. All of these can be wake-up calls. But, why wait for them? Why not live each moment you get with love, kindness, appreciation, generosity, compassion, gratitude, humility and caring?

Most of us are so busy trying to build a life, a career, a business or a relationship that we fail to notice that each of these is built either for the good or the bad - one second at a time.

What are you doing with your precious 86,400 moments today?

What will you do with them tomorrow? Next week?

-Indecision

One of the biggest causes of poor time management is indecision. It seals from your creativity while adding to your stress. Why do people fail to make decisions in a timely manner?

1. They fear making wrong decisions.

2. They believe it is necessary to always make correct decisions.

3. They don't have a system for learning from poor decisions.

4. They lack adequate information to make a wise decision.

5. They hope that decisions will 'eventually make themselves'.

6. They lack trust in themselves.

7. They have a history of poor decisions.

8. They see failure/mistakes as negative rather than the opportunity to learn.

9. They fear the future consequences of their decisions and their ability to successfully handle the outcomes.

10. They lack a systematic method for decision making.

Tim Connor, CSP

-Overcoming the fear of failure/success

If we are stretching ourselves, each of us fails sooner or later at something. It takes time to fail and it takes time to succeed. It takes energy to succeed and it takes energy to fail. Often the fear of success an/or failure finds its roots in our early childhood or life. We were engineered for success but often programmed for failure by our:

-caregivers
-schools
-friends
-siblings
-parents
-teachers

People who have a fear of success or failure will tend to waste time in routine or systematic ways. For example: a person who has a deep-seated fear of success will often sabotage themselves just as they are about to achieve a goal, objective or accomplishment. They will often do this by wasting time or unconsciously covering their territory or prospects in an inefficient way. These people usually don't see their personal blind-spots. Many people who are afraid of failure will never even attempt a task, objective or project. They will often spend their time in search of validation, approval or acceptance. Why not take a few minutes and answer the following questions.

How to Sell More in Less Time

1. Do you ever sabotage your success just before you achieve it?

2. Do you spend an inordinate amount of time in search of approval or acceptance?

3. Are you in touch with your personal blind spots?

4. When you are close to success are you able to reach inside for that extra "something" to succeed.

5. Do you have a habit of doing those things you fear or do you give in to them?

6. Do you persist when everything seems to go wrong?

-Self-discipline

What is self-discipline? Self – discipline is the ability to:

-stick with it until it: (whatever) is complete.

Tim Connor, CSP

-overcome personal tendencies to give in or give up.
-do what you know is right or best even when you don't feel like it.
-carry on when the odds are stacked against you.
-Your turn. How would you define it?
Sooner or later each of us has our discipline tested. Here are a few ideas to consider the next time you feel like quitting or stopping short of your goal or objective:

1. It is normal and natural to often want to quit. Everyone sooner or later feels like "what's the point".

2. Try giving someone in your life permission to hold you accountable to achieve your objective: (friend, peer, spouse, etc)

3. Remember: everything worthwhile takes time, patience and trust.

4. Play little accountability games with yourself.

5. Try pulling an all-nighter once in a while or not stopping until a project/activity is complete.

-The inability to say no

Is your plate so full that you don't have time for fun, family and friends? A common time management challenge for many people is their need to satisfy the demands, expectations and needs of the people in their lives; family, friends, peers, customers and fellow employees. This inability to say no often leads to increased stress, not giving adequate attention to your own issues, desires or activities as well as contributing to poor results in those areas where you do give your attention. The key is to know in what areas you

How to Sell More in Less Time

typically are unable or unwilling to put your own activities and demands first. Answer the following questions as honestly as you can.

1. Who in your life takes up the most time?

2. In what areas do you typically lack the ability to say no?

3. Which people are the most demanding of your attention and time?

4. Do you ever say yes when you really want to say no? With who? Under what circumstances?

5. When you say yes instead of no, how do you feel? About them? About yourself?

Tim Connor, CSP

-The self-image and time/territory management

How do you define your personal success? Is it about more, better, sooner, bigger or beating someone else? Or is it about achieving your own personal potential? Beating your own personal best? Is it happiness, wealth, education, achievement? Its your turn:

Success to me means:

Success is a very personal concept. It is different for each of us. Your self-image which was determined very early in your life (by age 10 at the latest) dictates:

-how you spend your time
-who you like to be around
-how you feel about others
-how you feel about yourself
-how you set priorities
-how you focus on challenges
-what projects/activities you complete
-how you respond to adversity, problems, failure, rejection and success
-how you negotiate

Your turn: what else is impacted by your self-concept?

1._____
_____

How to Sell More in Less Time

2._____

_____

3._____

_____

4._____

_____

For your consideration:

When you look in the mirror, listen to your own voice on a recording device, see yourself in a photo or video screen is your first reaction:

-I like how I sound, who I am.
-I could like myself better if…
-I will like myself better when…
-I'm really OK just the way I am.
-I don't need to change anything about who I am to accept and love who I am.

Or do you have opposite feelings or attitudes?

When you fail, is your first reaction,

-To blame others or circumstances.
-Take full responsibility for your own life outcomes.

When life gives you a problem do you,

-Look for an excuse or scapegoat.
-Adjust.
-Quit.
-Run and hide.
-Find another way to surmount it.

When someone says unpleasant things about you do you,

-Get angry at them.
-Listen and accept their view as theirs and it in no way is related to who you are.

When you receive a compliment do you,

-Make excuses.
-Thank them.

When you fail or life gets hard do you,

-Begin again.
-Never try again.

Time Tip

Only do critical tasks and activities that require creativity and imagination during your prime-time plus.

Tim Connor, CSP

When you succeed do you,

-Pat yourself on the back.
-Belittle your success.
-Pour it on.

When someone disagrees with you do you,

-Listen and learn.
-Argue and remain closed to new ideas.
-Act passively.

-Letting go of old emotional baggage

What is old emotional baggage?

Was it something your parents did or said 20 years ago? Something a customer said last week? Or something a spouse or friend said or did yesterday?

Old baggage is emotional stuff we carry around with us for days, months or even years. It is usually negative like old hurts, resentments, anger or some kind of pain inflicted by another person. It can also be just carrying around some old guilt, failure or fear that impacts our current relationships and life in general.

Why do people hold on to all of these old feelings? Everyone moves through life with their own very personal agendas, needs and life issues. Old baggage starts to feel very comfortable after a while, so comfortable as a matter of fact many people die never able to let go of these hurts, slights and pain.

How to Sell More in Less Time

There is one very good reason to let go of all of this baggage. One of the major causes of stress today is suppressed emotions that fester in the body taking their eventual toll on some aspect of our physiology. One of the biggest causes of stress today is all of this old baggage. So why let it go? It may kill you if you don't.

What is some of your old emotional baggage that may be sabotaging your effective use of time or your territory management?

-Decision making and choices

The ability to make wise choices and good decisions is one of the critical skills of all successful people. Every decision/choice you make has a consequence – some positive and some negative. Some long-term and some immediate. But, every action (choice/decision) has an ultimate outcome. The fact that you are reading this book is a result of thousands of previous choices you have made up to this point in your life. Every day your choices/decisions contribute each moment to each of your life; feelings, attitudes, beliefs, actions and results. Many people fail to make the connection between decisions and current circumstances. Your future success in sales will be the direct result of how you decide, what you decide and how or whether you follow through on those choices. Time use is a perfect example. Answer the following questions.

1. When you make a decision on how to allocate your personal or career time, you use (don't use) a strategy, set of guidelines or principles that contribute to your actions?

2. You typically make decisions: emotionally – logically – rationally?

3. You usually: think decisions over before making them – make them quickly - ask for input from others?

4. You thoroughly understand the concept of: decisions = outcomes?

5. You understand the: price (you pay) = the reward (you get) concept?

Control your thoughts:

One of the most critical skills for continued long term sales success is the ability to control your thoughts. Many salespeople let a variety of factors influence or control their conscious thinking activities. Some of these are:

1. Other people's behavior.

2. Circumstances beyond their control.

3. Past mistakes, errors etc.

4. Future, hopes, dreams and plans.

5. Internal frustrations with life, other people or circumstances.

6. The weather.

7. Present problems that have no immediate solutions.

8. Slights, criticism and judgments of others.

9. Invalidating remarks or actions of others.

10. Emotional game playing such as guilt, blame, resentment or anger.

11. Unrealistic expectations of life or people.

12. Career issues or the behavior, rules or policies of their organizations.

Just a few to ponder. Any of these getting in the way of your ability to maintain active conscious control of your thoughts and thinking patterns?

To be successful you MUST control those thoughts that dominate your consciousness. You must keep the vigil. Therefore be careful of the people you let into your life or surround yourself with. They are influencing what you believe, how you think, how you talk and how to behave and how you spend your time.

Tim Connor, CSP

Don't let anything or anyone have control over how you choose to use the most powerful, creative, awesome instrument you have at your disposal, your mind.

Giving power of your thoughts over to anything or anyone else is one of the biggest mistakes you will make that will have a lasting influence on your attitudes, life and destiny.

-Stress and time/territory management

Stress if it is not successfully managed will kill you. However, before it does it will steal from your time bank because it takes away your focus, creativity and the effective use of your unconscious imagination.

Stress is your inside-out reaction to outside-in circumstances, events or people.

Each of us daily, even hourly must confront people and issues that bring with them a great potential for stress. We can not stick our head in the sand and ask the world to go away. We must deal in the hectic, fast paced ever changing world of business and relationships. And we must survive as well as we can as we go about these daily routines. Most of us create our own stress and our stress reactions. We do so in a variety of ways.

1. We create unrealistic deadlines and expectations.

2. We set ourselves up for frustration and disappointment.

3. We have unrealistic attitudes and goals of ourselves and others.

How to Sell More in Less Time

4. We live out of balance.

5. We carry around blame, resentment and old baggage.

6. We suppress feelings and emotions.

7. But most of all we fail to keep all of this in perspective as we move through the days of our life.

So why do we do this to ourselves? And we do - do it to ourselves. No one does it to us. We do it in the name of success, financial gain, profit, competition, winning, more and more and more. And in the long run we end up with less. Less satisfying relationships, poor health, less fun, less happiness and less pure joy of living. Stress keeps you locked in the future or the past and out of the present.

If you are under stress you don't need this book to tell you. Your body is doing an excellent job of telling you this very minute. You are either ignoring the signals or overriding them with drugs, pills, aspirin, withdrawal, denial or other stimulants. There is something you can do to alleviate all of this stress in your life. Here are a few things to consider.

1. Lighten up.

2. Accept that life and business is a game. You win some and you lose some. You will never win them all and you won't lose them all.

3. Relax. You can not keep draining your battery without recharging it from time to time.

4. Slow down. You are not in a race. If you think you are, you will

never win it. Your only hope is to just try and finish, alive.

5. Stay in the present. Your mad dash into your future is all in vain. The time you miss now, the fun you miss now, the relationships you miss now and the simple pleasures you miss now can not be found in the future. They can not be enjoyed from a hospital bed or from the grave.

6. Laugh a lot. Laughter is nourishment for the soul.

7. Take time to play.

8. Accept people and life as it is. You can not change anyone. People are who they are and act the way they act. Period. Life is. You can not manipulate the rules of the universe and life to your liking.

9. Rest. It is not a sin to do nothing. It is not a crime to spend time in an aimless pursuit of nothingness.

10. Simplify your life.

-Self-evaluation and time/territory management

Honest feedback and self-appraisal is critical for change and lasting success. Each of us has a Varity of personal blind spots. If we fail to get in touch with some of these we can find ourselves:

-wasting too much of our time
-involved in time consuming repetitive activities
-spending too much time with poor prospects

How to Sell More in Less Time

-letting our prejudices color our attitudes, expectations and outcomes
-procrastinating
-avoiding difficult tasks or people
-staying in your comfort zone

Your turn:

1._____

_____

2._____

_____

3._____

_____

4._____

_____

5._____

_____

Now spend some time with the following to get you started toward better self-evaluation that will have a positive impact on your life and sales career.

Tim Connor, CSP

1. What does balance in life mean to you?

2. Do you feel out of balance in any area of your life now?

3. What is complicating your life now?

4. What or who are the biggest stressors in your life?

5. If they wrote a book about your life: What would the title be:

   -What is its plot or theme (comedy, tragedy, drama, documentary)

   -What is the title of the current chapter:

   -What is the title of the last chapter:

How to Sell More in Less Time

-What is the title of the next chapter:

-What do you need to do or change to make this an accurate forecast:

6. What or how do you need to change to simplify your life?

7. What would you like to change, but can't for some reason?

8. Describe your ideal life:

9. Do you have it now?

10. What do you need to change to make it so?

11. In what areas are you sabotaging your life or relationships?

12. What or who is getting short-changed in your life now?

13. One thing you would change in your life to be happier?

14. How would someone close to you answer these questions?

15. Are you willing to share your answers with them?

16. If you won a million dollars in the lottery today, what is the first thing you would do?

Why?

And the second?

And the third?

17. If you could live your life all over again, what would you change?

18. What are some of your biggest sales skills weaknesses?

19. Where does your attitude(s) need modification if you are to increase your sales success?

20. Where are you on your list of reasons for not doing well or better?

Tim Connor, CSP

-Sales slumps

Sooner or later every salesperson experiences a down period of sales results. These periods where your continued activity seems to yield less than satisfactory results are normal and to be expected. None of us can keep up a pace of 200 miles per hour day after day, month after month, year after year. The key is to keep your attitude positive, your focus on what is working, your activity levels high regardless of the results and to continue to manage your time and territory with the same passion, effort and effectiveness as if business was booming..

There are a variety of sales slumps. Here are a few.

1. An attitude slump.

2. A prospecting slump.

3. A presentation slump.

4. A closing slump.

5. A results slump.

6. An effectiveness slump.

An attitude slump is where you find it difficult to maintain your confidence, poise, commitment, dedication, persistence and motivation. This can be due to a number of causes. Some of them are: a) you have lost belief in your organization's products or services. b) you are not reaching your goals or objectives according to your schedule c) You are under a great deal of stress due to deadlines, expectations or loss of control of the sales process d) you have other issues in your life that are impacting your attitudes.

A prospecting slump is where you lack adequate qualified leads and are spending a great deal of time calling on poor prospects. As a result your close ratio is a disaster. This could also be caused by your poor prospecting strategies i.e. you are still (after several years selling your products/services) spending a lot of time cold calling.

A presentation slump can be caused by your lack of up to date product knowledge, poor presentation skills, or poor communication skills i.e. listening, speaking or writing. This can also be caused by your lack of knowledge of the prospect's needs, use of or applications of your products/services. You therefore give an organization driven rather than a customer driven sales appeal.

A closing slump can be caused by your lack of control of the sales process, poor prospecting, poor sales presentations, or many of the items in the attitude area we have already discussed.

As you can see there are a number of areas where you can experience a down cycle in your sales success. The thing to consider is that all of them are related to each other. In other words if you are experiencing an attitude slump it will have an impact on your prospecting, closing and time management.

The thing to remember is that you can't pull out of any of these slumps just focusing on the one area that you feel might be your problem. You have to work on all of them especially your continued use of time by not abandoning what you know, with time will one day soon yield successful results. The way out of a slump is to go back to what works, or has worked for you in the past in terms of activities, models, routines and processes. It is also an excellent time

Tim Connor, CSP

for reflection and self-evaluation of your progress, success, weaknesses and strengths.

All choices have consequences. Some are negative others positive. Some have short-term consequences while others are long-term. Make wise choices today.
They accumulate.

Tim Connor, CSP

-The Maslow hierarchy of needs and values

Years ago in the best selling book *Motivation and Personality*, Abraham Maslow put forward a theory that each of us functions in a level of belief, philosophy, or psychological need. His premise was that our decisions, actions, attitudes, behavior, beliefs and performance were a direct result of the level we were operating from. They are from the lowest to the highest:

The biological or the need for food, water, air, shelter.

The security/safety or the need to feel safe, secure and free of fear from the panic that comes when these are threatened.

The need for achievement. This is the desire or need to feel like we are accomplishing something that is worthwhile, challenging or satisfying.

The need for recognition. This is the desire to have other people recognize our achievements, successes, accomplishments as worthwhile and valuable.

The need for a healthy self-esteem. This is the first of the pure inside-out needs as opposed to the previous ones that are outside-in. When this level is reached the individual is primarily concerned with how they feel about themselves. Their drive is for 'good' feelings about who I am, what I am worth and where I am going.

The highest need – level according to Maslow is the need to feel self-actualized or that we are making a contribution to life, the planet, the good of Mankind. It is a total sense of inner peace, harmony and balance.

According to Maslow most people in society are functioning in the first four and very few ever reach the highest level.

How you use your time is a direct function of which level you are currently in.

Where do you think you are positioned at this stage of your life

Why?

-Develop a DO-IT-NOW philosophy

W. Clement Stone, one of the great success stories of the last century had a number of wonderful philosophies. One that stands out the most are his famous words: DO IT NOW.

Procrastination is a thief. It steals from many areas in our life such as:

-our relationships
-our careers
-our businesses
-our financial lives
-our happiness
-our success
-our lifestyle

Tim Connor, CSP

We are all on God's calendar. No one knows when they get up in the morning whether this will be their last day. And yet, many people put off: calling a friend, telling a loved one that they care, growing, learning and a host of other activities, behaviors and actions.

There is no benefit to waiting in most cases. Yes, there is a necessity for patience, faith and trust but the Quakers have a great saying: "Pray and while you pray, move your feet."

Life gives us two options when faced with a difficult challenge or problem.

1. We can do nothing.

2. We can do something.

Some of life's problems appear to leave us with few viable options. We always have a choice, an action we can take. We may not like some of them, but we do always have options.

What action, decision, objective, problem are you putting off today:

1._____

_____

2._____

_____

3._____

How to Sell More in Less Time

4. _____

Tim Connor, CSP

Chapter Summary...

Effective time use and territory management is a function of many factors the least of which are the attitudes, beliefs and habits you have formed over the years. I am confident by now you understand (if you completed all of the questionnaires in this first chapter) how complicated effective time and territory management is.

It is not just about a few tricks or making a to do list. You most likely wouldn't have invested in this book and the time thus far in reading it if you didn't feel you have some time and territory weaknesses or needs. If you answered all of the questions you should have a better handle on what these needs are. If you didn't complete them I can't recommend strongly enough that you go back to this chapter and take the time to seriously answer each of the questions.

You answers will become invaluable as you work through the remaining chapters.

I also recommend that if you haven't already done so that you purchase a three ring binder with eight tabs for your additional notes, questions and lessons learned as you move through the book.

Here is your first assignment:

After you have completed each of the exercises or questionnaires make a copy of them and put them in your binder. Spend whatever time necessary reviewing these to ensure they truly represent your feelings, beliefs, habits and attitudes.

How to Sell More in Less Time

"*If you are not ready today you will be even less so tomorrow.*"

Ovid

Tim Connor, CSP

Chapter 2...

Personal and career organization.

Overview:

Each of us has numerous demands on our time, energy and resources. One of the keys to sales success is the ability to balance multiple:

-demands
-expectations of customers
-requirements of our position
-tasks
-routine activities
-family roles
-personal needs and desires
-expectations of our supervisors
-personal growth possibilities
-and much more.

It is no wonder that many salespeople burn out early in their career due to the inability to successfully handle all of these issues, challenges and requirements. If success is one of your agendas you will ultimately have to:

-eliminate something from your plate
-better manage all of these issues and roles
-get better organized
-or live with the continued stress of poor organization

How to Sell More in Less Time

I am sure you know the feeling of being overwhelmed - the need to satisfy everyone and everything in your life as well as the desire to create a sense of peace in your life knowing that you - while working on other people's issues, expectations and demands - have not abandoned your own requirements for success, achievement and success as you have chosen to define it at any given point in your life.

You have also most likely known how you have felt when you have finished a day, week or month with a great deal of unfinished business. Everyone who hopes to do more, have more, become more, learn more and contribute more will, sooner or later, have to confront their own needs and style of what personal organization means to them. No one can tell you how to organize your life and career. What learning can do is help you identify where growth, change or a new philosophy is needed so you can regain some sense of harmony while climbing the ladder of personal success, whatever that means to you. Let's take a brief look at a few of the issues that will require your attention as you attempt to better organize your time, territory, career and life.

It is also important to know the difference between the words: effective and efficient.

-Efficient means to do things well or right.

-Effective means to do the right things well or right.

See the difference? It is one thing to end your day tired due to the business of completing your list of activities. It is another thing to end your day having completed the important things – those things that needed to get done, not those things you wanted to do because they were: easy, fun, you could finish them etc.

Tim Connor, CSP

One of the key characteristics in effective territory management is to do a better job of qualifying prospects prior to giving them your time, energy or corporate resources.

Let's look at a few ways to better manage your resource of time and territory management.

1. Ask more effective questions earlier in the sales process.

2. Pay attention to their answers to determine whether this is a good time to try and sell this prospect.

3. Develop a customer profile to use as a template for your prospecting.

4. Audit your sales call activity by dividing the number of calls you make in a week by the number of miles you drive in that week. This number will give you your call route effectiveness.

5. Spend more prospecting time getting referrals.

6. Develop strategic alliances to help you improve your prospecting activity.

7. Plan you call activities early in the week, month or day.

8. Don't give poor prospects more time than they deserve.

9. Get up earlier.

10. Go to bed later.

11. Use this extra time for planning, thinking or evaluating your

How to Sell More in Less Time

routines.

12. Develop a daily checklist of what you will need to do to be more effective.

13. Keep accurate sales records. The more information you keep the better able you will be able to spot potential trouble areas.

14. Try to get more of your prospects to visit your location, plant or office.

15. Don't spend time giving presentations to non-decision makers.

Even if you only do half of these, you will find your time will be better spent and you will experience better overall sales results.

-In the second column list all of your roles, responsibilities and business activities (how you spend your time)

Col. 1	Col. 2	Col. 3	Col. 4	Col. 5
___	_____	___	___	___
___	_____	___	___	___
___	_____	___	___	___
___	_____	___	___	___
___	_____	___	___	___
___	_____	___	___	___
___	_____	___	___	___
___	_____	___	___	___
___	_____	___	___	___
___	_____	___	___	___
___	_____	___	___	___
___	_____	___	___	___

If you need more space use your binder. You did buy one didn't you?

Now go back and review your list and determine which of these roles/activities are Revenue generating (RG) or revenue draining (RD) and indicate them in the first column.

Now estimate the total percentage of your time you spend in these activities/roles etc. Column 4. After you have completed this go back and categorize the list as an A activity: absolutely critical to your sales success. B: would be nice to do if you could and C: those are not critical to your success (third column)

Now project the new percentage of your time you would like (the ideal) to spend on these activities. Column 5.

Now ask yourself: can any of the B's or C's be eliminated or delegated.

-Paperwork

Paperwork is not going away, not in this lifetime anyway. It doesn't matter how technically oriented your organization becomes, there will always be paper reports; information to share, something to write, forms to complete, reports to evaluate or analyze and some piece of paper that finds its way to your desk or mailbox. The key is to honestly and effectively determine whether you want or need to spend time on this stuff or whether you can discard it without negative consequences. Let's take a brief look at a few of the paperwork demands on your time.

How to Sell More in Less Time

1. Expense reports

2. Call reports

3. Territory reports

4. Customer reports

5. Financial reports

6. Status reports

7. Customer history reports

8. Product reports

9. Forecasting reports

10. Goal or quota reports

11. Schedule reports

12. Competitor evaluations

Are you ready to march into your boss's office screaming – enough is enough!

Here are a few ideas to consider while managing paper.

1. It is a myth to believe that you can handle some of paperwork only once.

Tim Connor, CSP

2. Many of the reports you will submit to whomever, unfortunately, are not ever read. Let's be honest here, folks.

3. Technology will never replace someone's need or desire to have a 'hard copy' of something.

4. Let's face it – depending on who wants the information – a customer, your boss, a fellow employee or another department will determine your attention span and response time.

5. Most people are not good communicators on paper. They either go on and on and on with endless dribble OR they give us far too little information to help us make a decision.

6. Many reports are redundant exercises.

7. Many salespeople spend more time on paperwork/reports than they do selling.

8. Sooner or later someone/everyone wants to be copied on everything/something.

9. You need a priority system for handling your administrative tasks.

10. Some things can be delegated and some can't

11. File any notes you take during telephone conversations or appointments.

12. Keep only the articles from publications and not the entire magazine.

13. Establish a reading file.

How to Sell More in Less Time

14. Use expandable file pockets instead of hanging folders.

15. Keep your briefcase organized.

16. Bring blank letterheads, fax cover sheets, envelopes with you when you travel.

17. Delete old files from your hard drive.

18. Have an effective follow-up system.

19. Have an effective suspense action system.

20. Do difficult tasks first thing in the day.

21. Transfer to-do items to your planner.

22. Use a pencil for scheduling appointments.

23. Confirm all appointments.

24. Send yourself e-mails as reminders.

25. Leave yourself voice mail messages.

So, how can you streamline your paperwork?

1. Routinely allocate a specific amount of non-selling time to administrative
requirements.

2. Don't let paperwork/reports get in the way of you prime time selling activities.

Tim Connor, CSP

3. Make a daily/weekly appointment with yourself to reports/paperwork.

4. Categorize your administrative tasks into:

    -A- Must-do's now/today.
    -B- Should-do's now/today if you have time.
    -C- You will do when you finish you're A's and B's

5. Have a meeting with your supervisor to see if you can reduce or eliminate a particular task/report.

6. Form the habit of keeping daily records so at the end of the week it isn't as big a chore to complete a report or administrative task/function.

7. Organize you routine tasks reports/roles in such a way that they can be completed easily.

8. If you travel complete forms etc. while on the road in your hotel room rather than sitting in front of the TV.

9. Avoid useless surfing of the net out of boredom or just curiosity.

10. Delegate what you can to a subordinate, staff person or another department.

11. Have your mail screened by a support person.

12. Create files for your paperwork: routine, urgent, archive, action today, action this week, action this month, suspense, action this year, pending, to review, to read, when I get time, from my boss,

customer requests. Get creative here – the more you have the easier it is to keep track of everything.

13. Look for the summaries in reports.

14. Subscribe to a book review program.

15. Spend a half-day a week or month in the library catching up on industry information/trends.

16. Travel with your reports to review on the road at lunch or in the evening.

17. Listen to audio-cassettes of meetings while traveling.

18. Write responses on memos/faxes/e-mails rather than create a new document.

19. Keep things brief, short and to the point. Avoid editorializing.

20. Keep your memos, reports, correspondence accurate not perfect.

21. Use a dictating device that you can give copies to another department or staff person.

22. Develop a standard format or template for al of your routine reports.

23. Develop a follow-up system for your outgoing memos, requests etc. A contact management system like Act can manage all of this for you.

24. Have a self-rating system for how well you think you are doing

managing your paperwork.

25. Develop the habit of asking yourself: do I need to do this? Do I need to do it now? Can someone else do this?

-Keep Busy

Many salespeople waste a great deal of time. To be successful, you don't have to work 18 hour days, take work home with you on weekends, ignore your family and have no fun.

Just look at your personal work habits to see where you could be a little busier - not in busy work – but productive sales activities.

Hustle is not about working longer or harder for the sake of work.

1. It is about getting to a prospect before your competitor does.

2. It is about spending time in self-help s rather than in front of the TV every night.

3. It is about getting up an hour earlier every day to plan. It is about having breakfast/lunch/dinner with a client or prospect rather than eating alone.

4. It is about creating balance in your life so you have the will, energy and desire to put in the time necessary.

5. It is about working smarter not just harder. Although many people think that 'smart work' is a replacement for 'hard work.'

How to Sell More in Less Time

6. It is about spending time in reflection, contemplation and self-evaluation.

7. It is about managing your time in such a way that you maximize your results.

-E-mail

E-mail is a wonderful invention however it can also be a tremendous time waster. If you have an e-mail address everyone, even the spammers, will know it sooner or later. Checking e-mail several times a day can add up to an hour or more of your time. Consider the following:

1. Get off all or as many of the spammers lists as possible.

2. Get in the habit of checking your e-mail at certain times of the day only.

3. Download long messages for review at a later time.

4. Use the cc to forward or delegate messages to someone else.

5. Avoid sending/reading personal e-mails during selling time.

6. Use the telephone. It's faster than typing an e-mail message.

7. What can you add to this list?

Tim Connor, CSP

-Effective prospecting

One of the biggest time wasters is spending too much time with poor prospects who can neither afford or benefit from your products/services. It is important to have a prospecting strategy and/or philosophy if you are not going to fall into this trap of wasted time. The biggest time waster is when you fail to get adequate and accurate information about the prospect's needs, desires, dreams, problems, hopes, fears, challenges, concerns early in the sales process. The biggest mistake poor salespeople make is: they give information before they get it. When you do this you will tend to: give too much information, wrong information or inappropriate information. All of these sooner or later will waste your time either before, during or after the sales process is complete. Some of the time wasting prospecting strategies today CAN be:

-Cold calling

-Direct mail

-Socializing with prospects

-Trade shows

-Responding to requests for proposals

-Client meetings

Can you add any?

Here are a few prospecting questions to ponder.

How to Sell More in Less Time

1. Do you spend enough time with your best prospects/customers?

2. Do you let poor prospects steal your valuable time?

3. Do you have a prospecting prioritizing system that you use consistently?

4. Do you find yourself spending a great deal of time in after sales servicing issues?

5. Are you proactive or reactive in your prospecting?

6. Are you spending too much time traveling to and from your prospects?

7. Do you have a system for bringing new prospects into your pipeline?

8. Do you have a strategy for eliminating poor prospects from your pipeline?

9. Are you developing strategic alliances for new business?

10. Are you cultivating partnerships with other salespeople to improve your prospecting?

11. Do you have a NEXT philosophy?

12. Are you using technology as a tool or a crutch in your prospecting?

Tim Connor, CSP

-Prospect/client profile

A prospecting profile system is a simple yet effective way to always ensure you are in total control of your prospecting time. It is an approach that will help you maximize your selling time.

It works as follows:

You create a list of all of the traits/criteria for the ideal prospect/customer. You then prioritize these traits.

Next you determine which of these are absolute musts that a prospect must have, which ones you would like to have and ones you can live without. For example, let's say one of your criteria is sales volume potential. An A for you would be a prospect who can spend 100,000 or more in a year or per order. A B would be a prospect who could spend between $50-$100,000 and a C would be a prospect who could spend $25,000 to $50,000. Anyone who could not spend at least $25,000 would not be worth your time or effort. This first column:

A-

B-

C-

-Represents account status:

An - A = you know a lot about them/their organization – they know a lot about you/your organization and you are talking to each other. B = you know a little about them/their organization – they know a little about you/your organization and you are talking to each other.

How to Sell More in Less Time

C = you don't know much about them and they don't know much about you but you are talking to each other.

The second column of letters represents potential for new or additional business:

A-A

A-B

A-C

So an A-A would have high status and lot's of potential. An - A-C would have high status and not a lot of potential for new business.

-Now list all of the criteria to develop your profile.

-Now determine which make a prospect an A, B or C

-Next – determine the degrees, amounts or details that contribute to these classifications.

-Account allocation strategy

Here is the first question based on the above exercise:
How should you allocate your time to each category of prospect:

AA   BA   CA
AB   BB   CB
AC   BC   CC

Tim Connor, CSP

Here are three more:

-Which of the nine categories should get most of your time and why?

-Which of the nine categories should get the least amount of your time and why?

-What about the others?

Where are you on your list of reasons for not doing better, being happier or managing your time better?

Tim Connor, CSP

-Auditing territory coverage

The average salesperson who drives through their territory spends 0ver 25,000 hours in their career in their car. One way to determine the effectiveness of your territory coverage is to divide the number of miles you drive in a week or month by the number of calls you make. Let's say you drive 500 miles in a week to make 10 calls. That's an average of 50 miles per call. See if you can lower that number by making more calls or better scheduling of your appointments.

-Preparation

One of the keys to effective management of your sales time and territory coverage is proper preparation. So far we have discussed the mental preparation ideas that will help you succeed to achieve success in sales as you manage your time and territory.

It is also critical that you prepare your sales materials, presentations, resources and travel routines. Here are a few things that you might want to consider as you prepare for your next call or trip.

1. Are your materials professional, clean and organized?

2. Have you planned an effective territory coverage method?

3. Do you have all of the resources at your disposal you will need to have a successful call?

4. Have you confirmed all of your appointments?

5. Have you planned for contingencies?

6. Do you have a sales call or travel 'checklist'?

7. Have you confirmed reservations, transportation and trip details?

8. Have you anticipated any surprises that might impact your success?

9. Do you have a method of keeping track of follow-up committeemen's you make while on the road?

10. Can people reach you easily while you are on the road?

-Effective delegation and using support staff

You don't necessarily have to do everything yourself. If you have support staff, resources or other people in other departments who can assist you - effective delegation of routine or special tasks can lighten your load. A few things to consider when you delegate items to others:

1. Delegate results not methods.

2. Delegate authority with responsibility.

3. Set guidelines or parameters.

4. Establish rules for handling questions, uncertainty or problems.

5. Establish a schedule for feedback on progress up front.

6. Communicate expectations clearly.

7. Don't take the delegated activity back in mid-stream.

8. Trust the person you delegate to.

9. Give them permission to solicit help if they need it.

10. Remember – you get the behavior you reward. So reward results with recognition, praise or a simple thank you.

11. Don't' delegate revenue generating tasks/activities.

12. Don't delegate critical customer relationship building tasks.

-Travel

Many salespeople waste travel time in hotels, on airplanes, in restaurants, at airports, on turnpikes etc. The key is to maximize your time while on the road. Here are a few ideas that may help you.

1. Get a flash pass to speed up routine travel.

2. Bring reading material on the road (entertainment, self-help, business related)

3. Join an airline club.

4. Stay in hotels that offer Internet access.

How to Sell More in Less Time

5. Stay in hotels that provide business centers.

6. Tear articles out of magazines and bring them rather than the entire publication.

7. Use a lap-top computer while on the road.

8. Leave important contact telephone numbers with people who may need to reach you.

9. Purchase a cell phone. But don't use it while driving.

10. Use meals to meet with clients, associates suppliers.

11. Have someone review your incoming e-mails while on the road.

12. Use a contact management system that permits access to all necessary client/prospect information while traveling.

13. Read or write while on the plane.

14. Use a map software in the car or have current maps with you.

15. Get directions to your destination before you leave.

16. Confirm all reservations before you leave: cars, hotels, limo's, airline reservations.

17. Have a duplicate schedule with you while on the road and leave one with a spouse, associate, subordinate or friend.

18. Travel during non-rush hour periods.

19. Get up an hour earlier than usual while on the road.

20. When possible travel first class.

21. Get Cell phone caller ID.

22. Develop an office travel file which can contain: documents, itineraries, articles to read, information to review etc. Keeps everything in one place.

23. Use a journal while on the road to keep track of objectives, actions, messages etc.

24. Keep in touch with friends and family while traveling.

25. Have something in the hotel room that reminds you of home.

26. Stick with your typical routines while home such as: eating habits, exercise routines, reading etc.

27. Get plenty of rest.

28. Don't let delays, problems, uncontrollables, mistakes by others add to your stress.

29. Use electronic tickets.

30. Travel as light as possible.

31. Travel with only basic credit cards. Have a stash in travelers checks.

32. Get lap-top insurance.

33. Get in the habit of backing up your data.

34. Your turn. Add to this list.

-Voice mail

Technology is a wonderful thing. Voice mail gives salespeople the opportunity to reach their clients and prospects with information saving them time and energy. However, if voice mail prevents you from face to face or voice to voice communication you may miss opportunities to better service your clients. Technology in general is a positive thing, but not if it is used as a crutch and not a tool. Many salespeople leave sales messages, requests for returned calls and a variety of other information on this recorded wizard. Here are a few strategies in dealing with voice mail.

1. Never leave a sales message on voice mail for a new prospect that you have never spoken with unless absolutely necessary. If you must: keep it short, benefit centered and leave the information slowly.

2. Don't assume because a gate-keeper says your prospect is in a meeting that they are unreachable. Ask if they can be interrupted. You would be amazed how many times when you ask that question, how often you will get through to your prospect.

3. Don't assume, when you hear they are out of the office they can't be reached. Ask if they can be paged.

4. Don't ask people to return calls. Ask instead when would you

suggest I call back? The issue around call backs is that you lose control of the sales process.

5. When you leave a message for a call back with a current customer or qualified prospect, please leave your telephone number slowly.

6. Follow up the voice mail message with a fax or a hard copy of something. Some organizations still use paper and it takes more energy to throw away a message than hit the delete button.

-Prioritizing activities/time/tasks

Time Block Approach-

This strategy helps you blend the goals and objectives in your life with the available time at your disposal. It ensures that you don't neglect any area of your life while moving toward your goals and life purpose. It works like this:

You start with a month or week. You list your top five or ten goals in the important segments of your life in all or some of the following areas:

-Family
-Career
-Financial
-Social
-Education
-Physical
-Spiritual

How to Sell More in Less Time

First: Start with a clean month or week. Nothing included. Now take your number one priority – could be time with a spouse, exercise, reading, sales appointments etc. Block out the time for this area in the week or month. Now go to your second priority. Could be attending a social function or meeting. Continue to fill in blocks of time in your schedule according to your top goals, priorities or interests. As the week/month fills you now become acutely aware of how precious your time is and how you want/need to spend it.

If you do the month first now all you have to do is translate this information to your weekly or daily list of things to do. Another way to approach it is to take a year. Using the same philosophy, block out weeks, months or days for critical A, B C tasks responsibilities, activities and then get more detailed as you move from the year to a month, week or day.

This process ensures you don't neglect any important area of your life as you live it. Your career, personal life, financial concerns, social interests, family and personal needs get the attention they deserve.

Working from lists-

There is one sure way to ensure that you:

-don't forget to do something important

-work on the important stuff first

-will feel good about your day

-end the day/week/month without neglecting an important task, activity or role

Tim Connor, CSP

-have more fun

-enjoy the time you have

-can reduce the stress in your life

-get more satisfaction from your life's responsibilities

-will live longer

-will get more done

-can sell more

-will make more money

Work from lists of things TO DO. Here's how.

1. Male a list.

2. Prioritize the items on the list according to your goals, needs, desires, activities, demands etc.

3. Start with the important ones (must-do's) first.

4. Finish these before you move to the less important ones (should do's)

5. Finish these before you move to the unimportant ones (will do's if I get time)

This is not rocket science. Work from lists and you will get more done in less time.

-Quiet time

Life rushes on. Faster computers. More meetings. Tighter deadlines. Increasing demands on your time. More information at your disposal. Increasing responsibilities. The list is endless and ever changing. This rushing through life leaves little time for:

-planning
-contemplation
-reflection
-relaxation
-naps (and naps are good for you)
-fun
-thinking

Develop the habit of spending a certain amount of time each day/week/month and year in solitude or mini breaks for recharging your battery. It doesn't matter if it is walk in the park, slow relaxed meal, meditation time or just sitting doing nothing.

-Start a Journal

There are a number of outstanding reasons to keep a journal. Let's list a few of them. A journal can:

1. Help you avoid drastic errors in judgment.

2. Increase your effectiveness.

3. Improve your income.

4. Help you learn from your failures.

5. Improve your relationships.

6. Help you achieve your goals.

7. Keep you headed in the right direction.

8. Improve your lifestyle.

9. Help you learn from others.

10. Help you find peace and happiness.

11. Save you time.

12. Reduce your stress.

13. Help you have more fun.

14. Capture valuable memories.

15. Guarantee a worthwhile life filled with harmony, peace and joy.

Keeping a record of your insights, thoughts, ideas, successes, mistakes, errors, achievements and failures and their causes will do more for your career than any other single activity.

What have you got to lose. It takes less than 10 minutes a day to capture all of those important little day by day events, feelings and activities and their consequences that when re-visited on a regular

How to Sell More in Less Time

basis can have a galvanizing impact on your career, relationships and life.

Tim Connor, CSP

Develop a Do-It-Now Philosophy.

How to Sell More in Less Time

-Establish benchmarks.

If it isn't measured, it isn't happening. And you could be wasting lot's and lot's of time.

Establish benchmarks in your life to guide you consistently toward your goals. Benchmarks can give you a number of critical advantages as you move from one day to the next on your journey. Some of them are:

1. Accountability.

2. Re-commitment.

3. Re-evaluation.

4. Proper direction.

5. A measuring device.

6. Renewed belief.

7. Growing passion.

8. Integrity of purpose.

9. A warning sign.

Lofty benefits? Maybe, but critical if you want to achieve any measure of success and enjoy the success you achieve? Absolutely.

Tim Connor, CSP

A benchmark can be analogous to the road signs while driving on a long distance vacation to an area you have never been. It can also be a warning signal that something is amiss. If you are not careful you may never make it to your destination. Or you may spend extra hours lost looking for the right road.

Here are a few benchmarks to consider.

1. What are you going to do different this year than last to accelerate your progress?

2. What measurement guidelines do you have in place to ensure you are heading in the right direction?

3. What records do you need to keep to ensure you stay on track?

4. Who can you give permission to - to hold you accountable?

5. Do you have a plan B if plan A doesn't seem to be working?

6. Are you going to spend regular programmed time in reflection and re-evaluation?

7. Do you know where you want to go and WHY?

8. Do you know what you will do when you get there?

-Simplify everything

Are you feeling stressed, out of balance or missing some of the joy in life you feel you deserve or want?

How to Sell More in Less Time

Life can be a very complicated process. It is full of obligations, plans, goals, needs, expectations of others, problems, pressures, stressors, opportunities and A variety of projects, activities, and stuff in general. As you travel through life, you will discover that most people add to the already complicated nature of life with a number of emotional and physical attachments that inhibit a sense of balance, harmony and joy.

Simplifying life can range from an arduous task to a delightful process – it depends a great deal on what you want from life and what you may be attached to.

There are a number of books out today on the merits and virtues of the simple life. Some advocate moving to a small cabin in the woods without modern conveniences while others recommend cleaning out your closet.

What is the purpose and the benefits of simplifying life? This process can:

1. Reduce your stress.

2. Save you money.

3. Allow you to have more fun.

4. Give you more free time.

5. Increase your joy.

6. Permit you to enjoy the present moments of your life more.

7. Increase your harmony with others.

8. Save you time.

9. Lower your anxiety levels.

10. Reduce your frustration.

What can you do to simplify some areas of your life. These include but are not limited to your:

-home or living space.

-work area or business.

-relationships.

-career.

-interests.

-obligations.

-expectations.

-your needs.

-your routines.

-others (see what you can add to the list)

-You can't do it all in one day

No one can get everything done every day. Sooner or later you are going to have left-overs from the previous day. The key is to ensure those left-overs are not critical issues that require time that may become crisis's in the future. These can be eliminated with better planning and a time management system.

-The Value of good records

Have you ever experienced a sales slump? Or, just not achieved the results that you thought you should have? If you have been selling for at least 4-5 years most likely you have had some tough months or even a difficult sales year.

To determine where the problem is in a sliding sales career or poor month requires information. Information about sales ratios, actual numbers, trends, and comparisons. It is difficult to take corrective action if you are not aware of what is the cause of the problem or what actions to take. Just working harder or more hours calling on poor prospects is not going to have a significant positive impact on your overall results. It will be just more of the same.

Tim Connor, CSP

One of the common denominators, and there are many, among top salespeople is their ruthless evaluation of: activities, behaviors, time use, results and progress toward goals. Most poor salespeople don't take or have the time to keep accurate records.

Many sales organizations require call reports, but those reports are in many cases just busywork. They provide little if any value for the salesperson or the sales manager on where current or potential sales problems are or their causes. They just tend to require who did you see and what did you sell. This is not enough information if you are going to reach the stars as a salesperson.

If you are failing or are doing poorly do you know why. And, if you are consistently beating your goals, you have probably formed the habit of keeping good records and evaluating them on a regular basis to determine where changes in behavior is needed or new skills are required to continue to achieve.

-Contact management tools

One of the best time management tools is to use a flexible contact management system. Today there are several excellent software programs available.

-Act
-Goldmine
-Maximizer
-Sharkware

Whatever software system you use ensure that it can do most of the following for you:

How to Sell More in Less Time

1. Store an unlimited number of contacts.

2. Allow you to sort by any number of fields.

3. Mail merge letters to a select group of contacts.

4. Set up suspense follow-up activities well into the future.

5. Directly link to your e-mail program.

6. Modify field names and lengths.

7. Create special groups of contacts.

8. Schedule appointments, tasks and activities.

9. Create customer profiles.

10. Store and date detailed notes for each contact.

11. Surf the Internet.

12. Send and receive e-mails.

13. Give you a system of setting up to-do's and the ability to modify these lists easily and quickly.

14. Remind you of important dates/tasks.

15. Store and dial phone numbers.

16. Allow you to view a week, month or days activities/schedule/to-do's.

17. Write and send letters, memos and e-mails.

18. Create custom reports.

19. Link to other computers or hand-held devices.

20. Share databases with others.

Chapter Summary...

One of the best ways in sales to improve your use of available selling time is to develop a more effective system of prospecting. A monumental time waster is spending too much time on poor prospects.

Many salespeople erroneously believe that they can turn a poor prospect into a customer if they spend enough time with them. This just is not true. Salespeople do not determine the urgency needs, circumstances, problems, desires of a prospect – they discover them.

Once you discover you have a poor prospect as a result of effective probing, it is time to move on. Many salespeople today are also wasting a great deal of their time - cold calling. If this is your major prospecting method, I will personally guarantee you are wasting at least half of your sales time. Cold calling is no longer an effective way to prospect or spend your time. If you want to develop more effective ways to find, qualify and close more prospects I highly recommend you get and devour a copy of my first book, *Soft Sell*. Since 1981, over 500,000 salespeople have put the practical ideas for effective prospecting found in this international best seller.

One of the best ways to ensure you are prospecting effectively is to develop – an ideal client profile. Using this approach will guarantee that your valuable selling time is always in the presence of a good prospect: someone who can and wants to buy from you now or someone who is worthy of a certain amount of your time as their circumstances change and become more favorable for a future purchase.

Tim Connor, CSP

"First say to yourself what you would be; then do what you have to do."
Epictetus

Chapter 3...

Goals: (personal, career & business) as they relate to your Time and Territory management.

Overview:

-Success defined

What is success? That illusive yet sought after ideal that many people dedicate their lives to.

Success means different things to everyone. And it comes in degrees. For some it is a new toy, a positive bank balance, another meal, a dream home, financial independence, happy with their career, good kids, freedom of choice, and hundreds of other ideals and concepts.

Success is not about what we get as we travel through life but who we are becoming. You see, you will never have to worry about what you are getting in life if you will learn to focus on what you are learning and how it applies to how you are living. Success does in fact imply goals or a direction in life towards something. The value of these goals is not found in their achievement, but in the journey toward them. Goals are about direction. Life is about direction. Success is about direction.

Tim Connor, CSP

Many people say they want more success, but they can't get specific about what it means for them. Success is not about money, power, fame, wisdom, but the ability to live the kind of life you chose without interference or support from others. Measuring success is also an illusive concept. How do you measure happiness, well being, health or any of the other intangible objectives that many people have as their definition of success?

The search for greater success while leaving other important life areas in its wake is a mistake that many people make. What good is financial independence if you are terminally ill? What good is power if you are alone and unhappy? What good is fame if you are a prisoner to that fame?

You can never be happy where you are not, if you are not happy where you are. Reason - You have to take you with you into all of your future activities, relationships, businesses, career positions and so on.

Relax. Enjoy the process of your life. Before you know it will be over. Yes, work towards that which is important to you, but be careful not to sacrifice all your present moments in the process.

Action vs. intent

Intent is important, but your success comes from your action –what you do. It is important to have positive (good) intentions rather than negative (bad) ones.

-Some people are going to write a book for years, but haven't started yet.

-Some people say – some day I will……..

How to Sell More in Less Time

-Some people say – I would like to start my own business, but….

-Some people say they want to lose weight but can't give up that last french-fry or piece of carrot cake.

-Some people say they would – call, meet me at noon for lunch, send me something etc. etc. and they never do.

The real question is - are you guilty of any of them?

A few questions for you:

1. Is your word your bond?

2. Do you make promises to pacify people?

3. Do you do what you say you will do?

4. Do you let little roadblocks keep you from taking positive action?

5. Do you vacillate back and forth on what you want to do and why?

6. Do you talk about doing things to see how other people will react?

7. Do you talk about doing something to convince yourself?

To know and not do is to not know. Do not talk about what you are going to do – do it.

Tim Connor, CSP

-Motivation/success and goals

Motivation is one of the most personal issues there is. Research has concluded that everyone has the potential for great motivation, but not everyone is willing to pay the motivational price to achieve whatever their dreams, desires or hopes are.

A critical question that many people never really ask themselves is: what motivates me?

What are some of the traditional motivators:

1. Money.

2. Security.

3. Fame.

4. Power.

5. Prestige.

6. Ego gratification

7. Winning.

8. Being the best.

9. Doing your best.

10. Your family.

11. Your future.

12. Your past.

13. Not losing.

14. Personal satisfaction.

15. Approval of others.

16. To prove a point.

17. To get even.

18. To feel worthwhile.

19. To impress others.

20. To control others or situations.

Any of these drive you? Keep you going when you are on the verge of quitting, giving up or throwing in the towel?

Tim Connor, CSP

Time Tip

Ask yourself: Will my thinking about this or doing this have a positive impact on my life and/or career?

How to Sell More in Less Time

-Demotivators

For years - thousands of managers, hundreds of speakers and trainers and dozens of authors have been preaching the benefits and value of: Self-motivation and goals as a way to achieve success, wealth and happiness.

Let's look at de-motivators. A de-motivator is: anything - a person, or a circumstance - that acts upon you - and your interpretation of them or it and your subsequent behavior is negative, passive or self-destructive. There are hundreds of examples of de-motivators – here are just a few:

-negative people.

-people who invalidate you.

-people who don't listen, care or are interested in you or your thoughts or ideas.

-an incorrect personal interpretation of failure, problems and/or adversity.

-goals that are consistently too high or too low.

-managers who rely on fear and punishment as motivators.

There are, six basic steps to peak performance behavior and results when it comes to self-motivation:

1. Know what you want.

Tim Connor, CSP

2. Know why you want it.

3. Know how you will get it.

4. Know what may stand in your way to achieve it: (outside - circumstances/people/events or inside – attitudes/emotions/fears/doubts)

5. Become aware of the outside-in and inside-out de-motivators and develop a plan to deal with them, prevent them or manage them.

6. Do something. Begin. Start.

De-motivators come in all shapes and sizes. They can be your personal demons that no one but you are ever aware of or they can be a corporate policy or family rule that contributes to an – I don't care any more - attitude. Apathy is one of the most destructive human emotions when it comes to performance, productivity, happiness, success, motivation and overall behavior.

Conduct an internal as well as external self – audit of your de-motivators. Identify them, question their purpose and value in your life, decide if it is time to rid yourself of their power over you or - learn to live with the consequences of keeping them in your life.

One of the best ways to improve self-motivation and personal performance is to eliminate the de-motivators from your life, whatever form they take.

How to Sell More in Less Time

-Develop a goal philosophy

Even a goal to do nothing is a goal. Everyone has goals, they just define them move toward them or away from with a variety of perspectives or rationales.

There are two primary reasons for setting goals. First they give you focus. Second they give you direction.

Focus. Without focus it is difficult to hit a bulls-eye, take a good picture or avoid getting killed on a busy highway. Focus is an essential ingredient in successful people. They keep their eye on the ball. Yes, there are distractions, unexpected circumstances and unknowns that will impact your keeping your focus, but focus you must if you want to succeed.

Direction. The ultimate achievement of a goal is less important than the ability to continue working towards it. Many people achieve their goals and are disappointed once they get it. A goal once achieved is a milestone yes, but you can't just sit back and rest on your previous success. Even a shark will die if it doesn't keep moving forward.

When a winner doesn't reach a goal they reexamine what needs to change and then changes the time frame to achieve it. When a loser doesn't reach a goal, they re-examine and then change the goal.

Don't worry about the destination, keep your eye on the ball in the present with what you can do now, not tomorrow. Do something every day to move a little closer to your objective.

Tim Connor, CSP

You can't have everything in your life you want but you can have anything. Keep the understanding of this principle clear in your mind.

To set goals and not put accountability into the process is like whistling in the wind. You are living in fantasy-land if you think you will achieve your goals for this year if you have not made progress toward them and you do not have some benchmarks or checkpoints along the way.

Here are a few questions to consider:

1. Are you satisfied with your progress toward your goals?

2. If, not which ones are you behind on?

3. Why?

4. Are you ahead of schedule on any of your goals?

5. Which ones?

6. Why?

7. Is it time to let go of any of your goals?

8. Is it time to add some new goals to this year's list?

9. Who or what is affecting your negative goal progress?

10. Who or what is impacting your positive goal progress?

11. If you could go back to last year and begin this goal-setting process all over again would you have done anything differently?

12. What are you going to change in the next three months to ensure you are on target for your important goals?

Tim Connor, CSP

-How to set and reach your goals

Some things to consider as you go through this process:

1. Set time deadlines for your goals.

2. Know the difference between tangible and intangible goals.

3. Reward yourself when you reach a goal.

4. Update them at least every year.

5. Share mutual goals with other people who can help you, influence you or will be impacted by them.

6. Set both short (hourly – 6 months) and long term goals (6 months to lifetime goals).

7. Record your accomplished goals in a journal.

8. Be willing to abandon a goal when you have lost interest.

9. Accept the fact that patience and faith are virtues.

10. Know your reasons for wanting to reach a goal.

11. Relax and enjoy the process.

12. Life is not about the result, but the process of becoming.

13. Accept the fact that you can't do it all, have it all, learn it all, see it all, become it all, share it all in one lifetime.

14. Goalsetting is not a short term fix but a life time philosophy.

15. Life can change in a heartbeat.

16. Goals change as your interests, age and circumstances change.

17. Don't edit the goalsetting process as you proceed thorough the steps. (I don't have the time now. I can't afford it now etc.) Don't worry about being realistic in the beginning. The purpose of the process is to add realism as you go.

18. Goals should be achievable, but also require some stretch.

19. Get in the habit of working on paper with your goalsetting.

20. Recognize that achieving goals takes effort, commitment, time and skills.

Step One:

Create a list of everything you want to: do, see, learn, become, earn, spend, share, achieve for the rest of your life. Take as much time as you need. Take at least 2 hours for this exercise.

_____
_____
_____
_____
_____

Tim Connor, CSP

_____
_____
_____
_____
_____
_____
_____
_____
_____
_____
_____
_____
_____
_____
_____
_____
_____
_____
_____

Step Two:

Now take this list and transfer the items to the individual list where they belong:

How to Sell More in Less Time

Family

Career

Tim Connor, CSP

Social

How to Sell More in Less Time

Spiritual

Financial

Tim Connor, CSP

Health/physical/fitness

How to Sell More in Less Time

Mental/education

_____
_____
_____
_____
_____
_____
_____
_____
_____
_____
_____
_____
_____
_____
_____

Sales goals (New business, increased margins, Account penetration, Revenue, Retention)

_____
_____
_____
_____

_____
_____
_____
_____
_____
_____
_____
_____
_____
_____

You should now have 8 lists!

Step Three:

Prioritize the items on each list in order of their importance to you NOW.

Step Four:

Ask yourself a few questions:

   -Why don't I have it now?

   -What are my reasons for wanting it?

   -What will prevent me from achieving this goal?

   -Who could stand in my way.

How to Sell More in Less Time

Step Five:

Determine roadblocks to your success for each goal.

Step Six:

Now list some solution/action steps to overcome these obstacles for each goal.

Step Seven:

Establish target dates and feedback dates for each goal. (How am I doing)

Step Eight:

Get started.

Tim Connor, CSP

Time Tip

Use technology as a tool to better manage time, territory and relationships - not a crutch.

How to Sell More in Less Time

-Setting effective territory goals

Regardless of whether your territory is a metropolitan area or several states, the principles of effective territory management apply. The key is effective coverage of the geography you are responsible for. What does effective coverage mean? It is the ability to:

1. Get to your prospects before your competition sells them.

2. Spend adequate time with your best customers.

3. Cultivate positive relationships with your new customers.

4. Be responsive to customer problems, needs, issues and requests.

5. Become aware of new prospects in the territory.

6. Satisfy the expectations of your organization (boss).

7. Earn the income from your territory that you need to create the lifestyle you desire.

8. Have enough free time to pursue other non-career goals and objectives.

9. Reduce your stress due to ineffective coverage of your territory.

10. Achieve/exceed your quota for the territory.

Tim Connor, CSP

Here are a few questions to consider regarding your territory coverage and penetration goals.

1. Are you spending adequate time with your best customers?

2. Have you lost business due to your lack of time to get to current customers before you knew the business was in jeopardy?

3. Are the number of competitors increasing in your territory?

4. Do you have too many potential accounts in your territory to effectively cover?

5. Are some of your customers either requiring a great deal of your time or preventing you from adequate coverage of your geography?

6. Are your poor time management skills preventing you from effective territory coverage?

7. Are you spending too much time in travel to and from your customers/prospects?

-Common contributors to a lack of goalsetting success

1. Lack of commitment to the process.

2. Impatience.

3. Lack of follow through.

4. Lack of self-honesty.

5. Consistently setting goals to high.

6. Not anticipating roadblocks.

7. Not allowing for enough time to reach the goal.

8. Setting only long term goals.

9. Setting only tangible goals.

10. A lack of support, resources from people who can help you.

11. Working towards a goal you don't believe in or really want.

12. Not believing you will ever reach it.

13. Quitting too soon.

14. Not starting.

15. Poor records regarding your progress.

-Creating balance in your career and personal life

Balance in life means many things to each of us. There are entire books written on the subject. Here are a few of the critical factors in a balanced life.

1. Move consistently and purposely toward meaningful goals in all

seven areas of your life.

2. Live in the present - one moment at a time. The present is where your plans are made, memories are created and relationships built.

3. Live life from the inside-out, not the outside-in; taking full personal responsibility for the quality of your existence.

4. Let go of your old emotional baggage. It keeps you stuck in the past and prevents you from experiencing true joy in living.

5. Accept the fact that life just is! It is not perfect. Everyone has their share of pain, problems, disappointments, mistakes and struggles.

6. Daily count your blessings.

7. Live without regrets. Regret is a debt you can never pay. It will haunt you until your final day.

8. Make thoughtful choices. Choices become our ultimate destiny. Wise choices create a life worth living.

9. Live a simple and humble life. Keep your ego out of your actions, relationships, decisions and plans - you will find inner peace.

10. People, not things is what really matters. In the end it is not what you have accumulated that gives your life meaning, but people.

What would you add to this list:

Chapter Summary...

Recent studies have shown that less than 5% of the population regularly sets goals, writes them down and develops action plans to achieve them. Therefore just by developing a solid goal philosophy you place yourself in an excellent position to move successfully towards all of your dreams.

You would assume, at least I believe that if these statistics are anywhere near accurate that a lot more people who say they want to create a positive and rewarding lifestyle would spend a small portion of their available 24 hours a day setting and moving toward their goals.

There is a direct correlation between salespeople who have a clear goal philosophy and their effective use of time and their territory management. Show me a salesperson who sets goals, develops specific action steps to achieve them and I will show you a successful salesperson who manages their time effectively.

Without a concise goal strategy you are doomed to find yourself in the remaining 95& of the population whose actions do not match their stated desires. Success takes time. Learning takes time. If you fritter your time away in less than satisfying activities that keep you busy, but not moving you closer to your desires you are only kidding yourself.

Become a goalsetter today and watch how much more effective you become and how much faster you become the master of your time and your life.

Tim Connor, CSP

"Follow your dreams as long as you live, do not lesson the time of following desire, for wasting time is an abomination of the spirit."
Plato

Chapter 4...

Planning as it relates to time and Territory Management.

Overview:

There always seems to be enough time to fix things but never enough time to do it right the first time!

Effective time/territory management planning is critical in today's world of downsizing, restructuring and increased competition. It takes careful planning, execution and effective time use to spend adequate time to develop new business while spending enough time with existing customers to ensure loyalty, repeat and referral business. Research indicates that for every minute you spend in planning you can potentially save 10 minutes in execution. One of the biggest weaknesses of poor salespeople is their unwillingness and/or inability to plan:

-a new prospect strategy

-how best to prevent recurring client problems, issues or concerns

-how to spend the month/week/day

-how to develop/write a persuasive letter/proposal/campaign

-how to improve account penetration

Tim Connor, CSP

-how to increase margins

-how to sell around common price resistance

-how to sell more in general

Planning is the foundation of the effective salesperson's strategy. Knowing who to call, when to call, and how much time to spend with each prospect or customer is the starting point for success in sales. Most salespeople just "log" sales calls. They hardly ever have an overall strategy that guarantees effective territory coverage. The foundation for this planning is having enough information about the prospects status; i.e., knowing their potential for additional business, their willingness to give you that business and what their specific needs, problems, circumstances and expectations are. If you want to dramatically increase your sales, find out what is keeping your prospects up at night. What prevents them from getting a good nights sleep. This requires information, lots and lots of information. Next, Develop the habit of regular planning on a daily, weekly, monthly and yearly basis.

Execution. Knowing and not doing is the same as not knowing. Executing your plan requires flexibility, commitment, action, and follow through. Murphy's Law will get you every time. Expecting your plan to come off as "planned" is to be naïve. Expect problems, challenges, the inevitable last minute issue and uncontrolled events to sabotage your execution. Work alternative options into your planning. Plan for disappointments, setbacks and delays. This doesn't mean you are being negative, just that you are living in reality.

How to Sell More in Less Time

Your territory management plan also requires an effective call route strategy. This means determining the best call pattern to ensure effective coverage of your territory.

-Benefits of planning

1. Saves execution time.

2. Reduces stress.

3. Improves results.

4. Increased personal satisfaction.

5. Increased sales

6. Better territory coverage.

7. Greater success.

8. Better chance of goal achievement.

9. More free time.

10. Less waste of resources

Tim Connor, CSP

Time Tip

For every minute you spend planning, you will tend to save at least ten minutes in execution time.

How to Sell More in Less Time

-Consequences of poor planning

1. Repeated mistakes.

2. Wasted time.

3. Lost business.

4. Increased stress.

5. Vulnerable to the competition.

6. Wasted resources.

7. Lost opportunities.

8. Less success.

9. Reduced motivation.

10. Rushed projects/activities.

11. Fewer sales.

12. Lower margins.

13. Incorrect assumptions.

14. Misunderstanding.

15. Poor communication.

16. Others:

A planning model. Start with the end in mind

Most people who plan use history rather than the future as their model. To look back and arbitrarily assume that the future will be a direct extension or extrapolation of the past is to be naïve. The best approach to planning is to envision what you want the picture of the future to look like then work backwards from there.

-What to plan:

1. Sales approaches.

2. New prospect strategies.

3. Territory coverage.

4. Prospecting methods/strategies.

5. New revenue streams.

6. Margin/pricing strategies.

7. How to improve customer retention/loyalty.

8. How to win back lost business.

9. How to take business away from the competition.

10. What business to let go of.

11. Marketing and promotion campaigns.

12. How to competitor-proof your business.

13. Trade show participation.

14. Strategic alliance relationships.

15. New product introductions.

-When to plan:

All planning should be done prior to the time of implementation.

-The best time to plan Monday is on the previous Friday.

-The best time to plan next week is the previous week.

-The best time to plan next month is the previous month.

-The best time to plan next year is the end of the previous year.

-How to plan:

Planning does not have to be a complicated process as long as you have:

-a belief in its value

-commitment to results

Tim Connor, CSP

-time for the process

-focus/concentration while planning

-knowledge of resources

-awareness of internal and external threats

-the skills to create a realistic plan

-effective timing

-follow-through and follow-up

-inspection of the process

-accountability to the results

-flexibility when something goes wrong

-a willingness to learn

-a willingness to admit weaknesses, mistakes and shortcomings

Seems like a lot, but in reality if you have a commitment to the process you will learn as you go.

Here are a few steps to follow:

1. Set aside a specific time every day, week, month and year for planning.
    -20 minutes a day
    -an hour a week

How to Sell More in Less Time

   -a half day a month
   -1 day a quarter
   -1 week a year

2. Develop a planning template that you can follow regardless of whether you are planning a day or a year.

   -what
   -why
   -who
   -when
   -where
   -how
   -threats (internal & external)
   -resources
   -time involved
   -alternate plan
   -desired results

3. Commit the plan to writing.

4. Involve (communicate with) anyone/everyone who needs to know or can help you.

5. Stay flexible, in touch and keep your ego out of the process.

6. Hold yourself and others accountable.

7. Inspect the process and results regularly.

Tim Connor, CSP

Time Tip

Working smart is not a substitute for effort. The key is to blend the right amount of hard and smart work.

Chapter Summary...

One of the biggest time wasters is poor or inadequate planning. One of the reasons it is so difficult for many people to plan is that the concept of planning is such a nebulous task. It is not a concrete activity like making a list or qualifying a prospect.

Each of us has a unique approach to selling. Each of us is neither right or wrong in our approach. The only measure as to whether your system, philosophy or approaches are effective is: ARE YOU MAKING THE KIND OF INCOME YOU WANT AND FEEL YOU ARE WORTHY OF? In sales there is no other standard. Yes, the number of referrals you get, the percentage of repeat business, your average margins per sale etc. are all benchmarks. However, the bottom line is how well are you doing financially?

Planning involves a great number of activities from planning a sales call, your day to a long-term strategic approach to taking business away from a competitor.

The best way to develop a planning system that will consistently work for you is to make planning a PRIORITY - in your day, week, month and year. Yes, these plans need to be flexible, dynamic, responsive and realistic but don't let these criteria prevent you from getting started with a planning approach that helps you chart a more effective future.

The process is not rocket science. All that is involved to become a better time manager is to: Know your attitudes and tendencies, set goals, put these into plans of action and then get started. I just summarized the 150 plus pages in this book.

Tim Connor, CSP

Chapter 5...

Common time and territory wasters and stretchers.

Overview:

THE FOLLOWING IS A CHECK-UP ON WHAT YOU HAVE LEARNED THUS FAR.

See how many reasons, excuses, challenges, or problems you can come up with that affect the poor use of time and then list at least 3 ideas to overcome or deal with the issue.

-Unrealistic time expectations

-Un-managed stress

-Time management attitudes/philosophy

-Lack of goals

-The Internet

-Poor organization

-Not having a time management strategy

-Low self-esteem

-Technology

-Poor decision making

-Lack of delegation

-Lack of planning

-Procrastination

-Doing the easy stuff first

-Poor prospecting

-Poor travel scheduling

-The telephone

-Customers

-Fellow employees

-Poor communication

-Socializing

-Your boss

-Administrative tasks

-Poor territory management

-Other departments

-Poor sales skills

-Poor personal management/organization

-Interruptions

-Paperwork

-Repetitive tasks

Tim Connor, CSP

-E-mail

-Meetings

-Poor preparation

-Mail

How to Sell More in Less Time

-Call backs and voice mail

-The telephone

-Others: (Here is where you can add items to the list – if you feel like it.)

1._____

2._____

3._____

4._____

5._____

6._____

7._____

8._____

9._____

Tim Connor, CSP

Chapter Summary...

What did you learn in this chapter?

Chapter 6...

Technology and time and territory management.

Overview:

Technology can dramatically improve you time and territory management. However, it can also increase your stress and wasted time. How, you ask? Surfing the net, searching for information among the millions of websites and getting hundreds of e-mails a week all takes time. Time away from selling. And, time away from other revenue generating activities. It can also be hazardous to your health. Recent research has indicated that people using a cell phone while driving have a 65% greater chance of having an accident than those of us who have chosen to invest in cell phones but use them more responsibly.

-Use technology as a tool not a crutch

Questions:

-You can e-mail a customer or call them. What is your best option for improving the relationship?

-You can surf the net on your laptop during lunch or you can have lunch with a prospect? Any thoughts?

Tim Connor, CSP

-You can visit a customer while in their area or you can call them on your cell phone? What do you think?

The general rule of thumb is to follow the following guidelines.

1. Don't assume your prospects/customers are as technologically advanced or sophisticated as you are.

2. When in doubt call rather than e-mail someone unless they have told you they prefer e-mail.

3. Use the Internet as a business tool primarily to help you save time when researching client/prospect/industry information.

4. Direct people to your organization's website (if you have one) only as a secondary option to a personal visit.

5. Be more knowledgeable about your prospect's business than your competition.

- Now it's your turn:

-Latest software

_____
_____
_____
_____
_____

How to Sell More in Less Time

-Latest hardware

-Newest toys

Tim Connor, CSP

-Most recent technology

-Relevant websites

How to Sell More in Less Time

Conclusion...

Your personal action plan

Overview:

Now it is time to put into practice what you have learned. It is time to develop your personal action plan. Use your binder for this section.

1. Personal actions you will take during the next 30 days as a result of this book.

2. Time habits you believe you may have that are sabotaging your sales success.

3. A scheduled process (so many hours per week/month) where you will constantly evaluate your on-going progress in time/territory management improvement.

That's it folks. Now, get to work...

-As a result of this book, I plan to Take the following action steps in the next 45 days:

1.

2.

3.

4.

5.

6.

7.

8.

9.

10.

11.

12.

13.

14.

15.

16.

17.

18.

19.

20.

Tim Connor, CSP

-Recommended Reading

As a Man Thinketh, Allen

Acres of Diamonds, Conwell

Richest Man in Babylon, Clason

Life is Tremendous, Jones

The Greatest Salesman in the World, Mandino

The Ancient Scrolls, Connor

Selling Leverage, Exton Jr.

Try Giving Yourself Away, Dunn

Jonathan Livingston Seagull, Bach

Soft Sell, Connor

Think and Grow Rich, Hill

The Three Keys to Success, Beaverbrook

The Road to Happiness is Full of Potholes, Connor

The Greatest Secret in the World, Mandino

Sales Mastery, Connor

The Power of Positive Thinking, Peale

How to Sell More in Less Time

Will the Real Me Please Stand Up, Powell, S.J.

Time Power, Rutherford

Psycho-Cybernetics, Maltz

The Magic of Thinking Big, Schwartz

Man's Search for Meaning, Frankl

Focus or Failure, Amos Jr.

Wake Up and Live, Brande

The Magic of Believing, Bristol

Do What You Love and the Money Will Follow, Sinetar

Time Trap, MacKenzie

Fully Human, Fully Alive, Powel, SJ

The Kingship of Self-Control, Jordan

I Dare You, Danforth

47 Ways to Sell Smarter, Meisenheimer

How to Sell More With Less Rejection, Sobczak

Do Less, Achieve More, Chu

50 More Ways to Sell Smarter, Meisenheimer

Tim Connor, CSP

Please Understand Me, Kiersey/Bates

The Trade-Off, Connor

Transitions, Bridges

"You will be the same person in five years you are today except for the books you read and the people you meet!"

"Your work may be finished someday, but your education, never."
Alexandre Dumas

Tim Connor, CSP

Tim's most popular Seminar Topics...

Sales and Customer Service

Customer focused selling strategies
Peak performance selling
Time and territory management
How to differentiate yourself in a competitive marketplace
How to increase sales and customer loyalty in a changing world
Effective customer service strategies
Advanced customer service techniques

Personal and Career Development

The Road to Happiness is Full of Potholes
The power of personal motivation
Setting and reaching goals
Effectively managing stress and burnout
Effective communication skills
Managing life's transitions
Achieving balance in life and your career

Relationship Strategies

How to build and maintain positive sales relationships
Relationship strategies for vendors, dealers, franchisees or distributors
How to empower employees for improved productivity
How to manage conflict
Creating win/win relationships

Management and Leadership

Effective leadership
Improving organization communication
How to support not sabotage employee performance
Strategic planning for top managers
How to find, interview and select the best employees

To discuss Tim's availability and fees to conduct one of these or other custom programs for your organization please give Tim a call at: 800-222-9070.

How to Sell More in Less Time

Tim's most recent book...
The Road to Happiness is Full of Potholes...

Happiness! Everyone wants it, searches for it, dreams of it and longs for it. Are you happy? Really happy? If so, why? If not, what will it take for you for once and for all find and keep this illusive yet seemingly attainable life?

I have been miserable. I have been happy. And, I have spent time in that limbo state of wanting to be, but not knowing how to find it.

Happiness is not a thing, address, possession, bank balance, life position (retirement, married, single, parent, etc.). It is not something you can grasp, earn, keep, buy, learn, give away or know. Happiness is not anything that you go after. It will come after you relentlessly if you have that inner mental state or consciousness that says, I am happy no matter what is in my life.

This does not mean to imply that you will be happy 24 hours a day 365 days a year. That would not be life as it was designed to be, it would also be exhausting. However, we were meant to be happy as a life destiny. Pain, grief, sadness, solitude and yes even loneliness are all valuable contributors to a humble, joyous, compassionate, loving, balanced, happy and productive life.

You cannot totally experience the thrill of victory without ever tasting defeat. You cannot completely bask in the sunshine of success if you have never been brought to your knees. And, you cannot know fully the joy of a happy disposition, spirit and demeanor without ever knowing unhappiness.

This is a thought-provoking, entertaining and wonderful book about how to find lasting happiness in all areas of your life. Only $11.95.

Tim Connor, CSP

The Trade-Off, a new fiction self-help story from Tim...

Jason pleaded with his well-conditioned legs to carry him just a hundred more yards. He knew the terrain, so he was able to look back over his shoulder every few seconds to see if he was gaining on him. Sweat was pouring off his face. His shirt and shorts were soaked with the sweat of several hundred yards of nonstop sprinting. He was operating now on pure adrenaline. Although he was the state champion in the one hundred-yard dash for the past four years, he never had to run for his safety in his dozens of races. He ran because he loved to run. Now, he was running for his life.

He was gaining on him. Just forty more yards to safety. Would Jason make it this time? Thirty, twenty, ten. He was now within arms reach. Five... Jason could feel his ugly breath on his neck, like the hot summer wind.

"I made it." And then he collapsed.

Jason could hear the soft, gentle voice call to him as if it were a million miles away.

"Jason! Jason, wake up, it is time to get ready for school."
"Mom, is that you?"
"Yes, son. Who were you expecting?"

The dream was as fresh in his mind as if he had actually lived through the chase just moments earlier. This was a recurring dream for him. And yet each time there was something different about the dream. He couldn't quite put his finger on it, but he knew that one night soon, he would not make it to safety.

Available now... only $15.00.

How to Sell More in Less Time

"May you live all the days of your life."

Jonathan Swift

Titles available from: Connor *Resource* Group

Mail orders: Tim Connor, CSP, Connor Resource Group, Box 397, Davidson, NC 28036 USA
Tel. Orders: (800) 222-9070 • (704) 895-1231 • Fax Orders: (800) 222-9071 • E-Mail: speaker@bellsouth.net
Website: www.timconnor.com

BOOKS AND MANUALS	Price	Ship	Take	Amount
The Trade-Off	15.00			
Sales Mastery	24.95			
How to Sell MORE in LESS Time	20.00			
Soft Sell (paperback)	12.95			
52 Network Marketing Tips	8.95			
Daily Success Journal	45.00			
Success Journal (30 day trial version)	7.50			
The Voyage	15.00			
The Road to Happiness is Full of Potholes	11.95			
The Road to Happiness Fun Book	5.95			
Win-Win Selling (E-Book)	19.95			
The Ancient Scrolls	15.00			
Success Book Club	$85.00			
Tim's weekly E-Mail Tips (Mgt., Sales, Motivation, Relationships, Success)	25.00 Topic/ YR			
Assignment Workbooks .... (Set of 5 Workbooks)	85.00			
• Sales Assignment Workbook	19.95			
• Management Assignment Workbook	19.95			
• Relationship Assignment Workbook	19.95			
• Customer Service Assignment Workbook	19.95			
• Success Assignment Workbook	19.95			
Life Balance Newsletter (12 issues)	96.00			
AUDIO CASSETTES	Price	Ship	Take	Amount
Soft Sell Sales Courses	195.00			
Sales Development Skills	70.00			
Personal Development Skills	70.00			
Management Development Skills	70.00			
The Road to Happiness Audio Series	20.00			
Master Speakers Int'l Beating Your Competition	85.00			
Soft Sell Mini Cassette Album	25.00			
Search (8 cassettes)	85.00			

PAYMENT METHOD

☐ Enclosed is my check for $_____
☐ Charge my: VISA/MC/Amex/Discover
  $_____
No: _____
Exp. Date: _____
Signature: _____

SUBTOTAL $_____
(ADD SHIPPING) $____**5.00**
Prices are quoted in US Funds
TOTAL $_____

TO ORDER - Please Print Clearly

Name: _____
Tel No. _____
Org.: _____ Email: _____
Address: _____
_____
City: _____ State: ____ Country: _____ Zip: _____

☐ Please send information on Tim's services as a keynote speaker, trainer and/or consultant.